THINGS TO MAKE
AND DO FOR
THANKSGIVING

A THINGS TO MAKE AND DO BOOK

THINGS TO MAKE AND DO FOR THANKSGIVING

by Lorinda Bryan Cauley

FRANKLIN WATTS
NEW YORK/LONDON/1977
FIELDS CORNER

Library of Congress Cataloging in Publication Data

Cauley, Lorinda Bryan.
  Things to make and do for Thanksgiving.

  (A Things to make and do book)
  SUMMARY: Includes a history of Thanksgiving, crafts,
recipes, jokes, riddles, and games relating to this
holiday.
    1. Thanksgiving decorations—Juvenile literature.
2. Thanksgiving Day—Juvenile literature.
[1. Thanksgiving Day. 2. Thanksgiving decorations.
3. Handicraft] I. Title.
TT900.T5C38   745.59′41   77-24833
ISBN 0-531-01324-3

Thanksgiving is the fourth Thursday in November.

Before dinner, you can make some name cards out of leaf rubbings.

To make 4 name cards, you need:

1 piece of typing paper
3 crayons
Scissors
4 dry leaves

Then put one at each person's place around the table.

How to do it:

1. Fold the paper in half. Cut along the fold.
2. Now fold these two pieces of paper in half. Cut along the fold.
3. You now have four pieces of paper. Fold each in half. Put a leaf inside each piece of folded paper.

4. Rub a crayon gently across the front of each piece of folded paper. The outline and veins of the leaves will show.

You need:

Plate
Big lettuce leaf
Big apple
8 toothpicks
12 cranberries
20 raisins
A marshmallow
Scissors

An apple-turkey statue is fun
to make for the center of the table.

How to do it:

1. Put the lettuce leaf on the plate. Place the apple on top.
2. Take 4 toothpicks. Stick 3 cranberries on each.
3. Take 3 more toothpicks. Stick 5 raisins on each.
4. Poke the 7 toothpicks into one end of the apple for a tail.
5. For the neck, stick 3 raisins on the last toothpick.
6. Take your scissors. Snip one edge of the marshmallow for a beak—like this.

7. Press a raisin into each side of the marshmallow for eyes. Push the marshmallow on top of the neck.
8. Poke the neck into the other end of the apple.

After dinner you can "gobble, gobble" it all up.

Here is a good dessert to make for Thanksgiving dinner. It is one the Pilgrims used to eat—Indian pudding.

For 6 to 8 people, you need:

1 quart of milk
¾ cup of molasses
1 cup of cornmeal
½ stick of butter
2 tablespoons of sugar

½ teaspoon of salt
¼ teaspoon each of nutmeg, cinnamon, and ginger
2 beaten eggs
1 teaspoon of shortening
1 saucepan
1 spoon
1 baking dish

How to do it:

1. Heat the milk in a saucepan.
2. Add the molasses and cornmeal to the milk. Stir until it is all mixed together. Now boil.
3. Remove the pan from the heat. Add the butter, sugar, salt, nutmeg, cinnamon, and ginger. Cool for about 10 minutes.
4. Stir in the already beaten egg.
5. Grease the baking dish with the shortening.
6. Pour in the pudding.
7. Bake at 325° for an hour.

In the 1600s, the Indians ground corn by pounding it between two stones. Their name for corn was "maize" (mayzzz). This means "bread of life" or "grain of the gods."

They made molasses by crushing sugar cane. Then they boiled it in a pot until it was a thick, sweet syrup.

Indian pudding is good hot or cold.

Top it with ice cream or yogurt if you like.

After dinner is a good time to tell jokes.

After dinner, you can also make Indian belts. The Indians used dyed porcupine quills and wampum. Wampum is a string of polished beads.

You need:

1 large piece of thick paper
Ruler
Sharp pencil
Scissors
Tape
Box of crayons
2 pieces of colored yarn
   as long as your arm

How to do it:

1. Take the paper. Lay it down lengthwise.
Measure two 3-inch-wide strips.
Cut out each strip like this.

2. Tape the strips together like this.

3. Wrap the long strip around your waist.
Mark the spot where the ends
touch with your pencil.
Now add on about two extra inches.
Cut off the rest like this.

4. Take your pencil and poke two holes
in the end of each strip like this.

5. Color a nice design around the belt.
The Indians often drew birds, deer,
flowers, trees, or simple shapes.

6. Take one piece of yarn. Push it through
the holes at one end of the belt like this.

7. Do the same with the other piece of
yarn at the other end of the belt. Now
tie the belt around your waist like this.

Paper feathers are fun to make.

The Indians near Plymouth, Massachusetts, wore one or two eagle feathers in their hair —not big warbonnets. An eagle feather is white with a dark brown tip.

For two eagle feathers, you need:

2 pieces of white paper
2 pencils
Scissors
Tape
Glue
Brown crayon
A piece of yarn twice as long as your arm

How to do it:

1. Draw two big feathers on one piece of paper like this.

2. Put the two pieces of paper together. Cut out the feather shapes. You now have four feathers.

3. Take two of the feathers. Place a pencil in the middle of each. Leave room at the bottom like this.

4. Tape the pencils in place.

5. Glue the other two feathers on top. Let them dry.

6. Take the brown crayon. Color the tops of the feathers.

7. With the scissors, snip the edges all around the feathers like this.

8. Tie the yarn around your head twice. Stick the two feathers in the back.

Indians sometimes talked with their hands. Here is something you can say using their signs.

MUCH—Hold your hands like this.

Bring your hands down and together like this.

Now lift them up.

RAIN—Make two fists. Now hold them in front of your shoulders like this.

Lower your fists slowly, while opening your fingers. Do this a few times to show rain.

HELP—Hold your palms so they face each other like this.

Move your hands up and down, past each other, like this.

Put the index finger of your right hand against your left palm like this.

CORN—Hold the thumb and index finger of your left hand with the thumb and index finger of your right hand like this.

Turn your right hand a few times like this.

GROW—Hold your right hand near the ground with your finger pointing up like this.
Move your hand up in short jerks.

Here's a sentence that is fun to say.

WE—Point to yourself with your thumb. Starting with your right shoulder, move your hand—palm down—in a flat circle like this.

EAT ENOUGH—Cup your right hand like this.

Move it up and down in front of your mouth. Now spread your thumb and index finger. Move your hand up from your chest to your chin like this.

THANK YOU—Hold both hands shoulder high, palms out, like this.

Push them down and away from you like this.

Feather Relay is a good game to play after dinner.

You need:

2 fluffy feathers *or*
  2 small balloons
2 pieces of string 8 times
  as long as your arm
8 players or more

How to do it:

1. Make two teams of players
—Team A and Team B.
2. Put two strings on the floor
about 12 paces from each other.
3. Divide each team in half. Have
one half of Team A stand behind
one string. The other half of
Team A stands behind the
other string. Do the same
thing for Team B.

4. On "Go" the first player from each team must blow a feather across the room to a teammate. If the feather falls to the floor, the player must pick it up and keep going.

5. The teammate must then blow the feather back across the room to another teammate. Every team member must have a turn.

6. When the last player on a team is done, the whole team sits down. The first team sitting wins.

Another good Indian game is Toss and Catch.

You need:

2 pieces of cardboard,
   each 5 inches square
A long pencil
Scissors
Tape
Glue
Felt-tip pens in different colors
4 pipe cleaners
2 pieces of yarn, each
   as long as your arm

How to do it:

1. Draw a big circle on each piece of cardboard. Make sure the circles are the same size. Now cut them out.
2. Take the pieces of cardboard that are left and cut out two horns.

3. Take one of the circles. Tape the pencil to the edge of it like this.

4. Tape the horns to it like this.

5. Glue the other circle on top—with the pencil and horns in the middle.

6. Color a bull's head or Indian design on each side.
7. Poke a hole in the top—between the two horns—like this.

8. Take two pipe cleaners. Twist them together to make one long pipe cleaner. Bend this into a ring. Twist the ends together like this.

9. Take one piece of yarn. Tie it to the ring like this.

10. Tie the yarn and the ring to the bull's head like this.

11. Hold on to the pencil and jiggle the bull's head so the ring lands on one of the horns.

12. When you get good at catching one ring, take the other pipe cleaners and make another ring. Tie it to the bull's head with the extra piece of yarn. Now try to catch both rings at the same time!

Here is a good guessing game to play with your family and friends.

BEET has it but CORN does not.

TREE has it but LEAF does not.

FALL has it but WINTER does not.

ROOSTER has it but TURKEY does not.

What is it?

The answers are on the last page.

On Thanksgiving it is also fun to make Radish Finger Puppets.

You need:

10 big radishes
A small knife or apple corer
A black felt-tip pen
Poster paints
A small brush

How to do it:

1. Take the knife or apple corer and make a hole in the fat end of each radish. The hole must be big enough to fit your finger in.
2. Use the pen to draw a face on each radish.

3. With poster paints, make five of the radishes look like Pilgrims and five of them look like Indians.
4. Put one radish on each finger. Now you can give a puppet show about the first Thanksgiving.

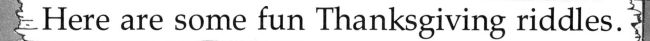

Here are some fun Thanksgiving riddles.

Round as an apple.
A color like gold.
With more things inside,
Than you are years old.
What is it?

A Pilgrim had nine ears of corn in his barn. Each day a squirrel came to the barn and took away three ears. But it took the squirrel nine days to remove all the corn. Can you guess why?

An Indian had 2½ piles of corn in one row. He had 1½ piles of corn in another row. Then he put them together. How many piles did he have?

The Indians used picture writing to tell stories. They made colors from dirt, grass, plants, and flowers. Their brushes were made of buffalo bone. Picture writing is good for secret messages. Here are some pictures the Indians used.

TALK TOGETHER

AUTUMN

GOING TO A FEAST

GREETINGS

MUCH (HEAP)

STAR

HONEST

MEET

LIGHTNING

ALL

PERIOD

PEACE

CATCH

LEAF

FISH

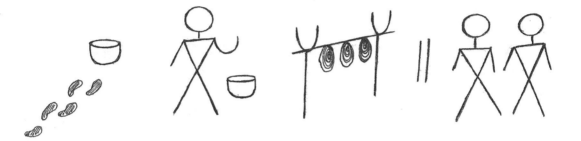

The answer is on the last page.

Answer to the puzzle on page 13:

Answer to the guessing game on page 39:

All of the first words have double letters in them.

Answers to the riddles on pages 42 and 43:

A pumpkin.

The squirrel took away three ears, but only one was made of corn. The other two were his own.

One.

Answers to the mixed-up dinner on page 43:

1. Squash
2. Corn bread
3. Stuffing
4. Sweet potatoes
5. Gravy
6. Pumpkin pie
7. Roast turkey
8. Indian pudding
9. Green beans
10. Cranberry sauce

The picture writing on page 46 says:

In late November we will all go to a feast and eat plenty of food. We can talk together and dance and be happy.